C000186470

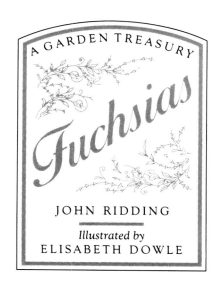

A GARDEN TREASURY

Fuchsias

JOHN RIDDING

Illustrated by
ELISABETH DOWLE

HarperCollinsPublishers

First published in 1994 by
HarperCollins Publishers, London

Created exclusively for HarperCollins by Clare Clements

Text © John Ridding 1994
Illustrations © Elisabeth Dowle 1994
All rights reserved

John Ridding asserts the moral right to be identified
as the author of this work

Designer: Clare Clements
Editor: Caroline Taylor

For HarperCollins Publishers
Commissioning Editor: Polly Powell
Project Editor: Barbara Dixon

A CIP catalogue record for this book is available
from the British Library

ISBN 0 00 412958 X

Typeset in WTC Goudy by SX Composing Ltd
Colour reproduction in Singapore by Colourscan
Printed and bound in Italy

'A most beautiful ornament when well grown.'
WILLIAM ROBINSON, 1883

ACKNOWLEDGEMENTS
Clare Clements would like to thank Norah Varley,
and Elisabeth Dowle would like to thank Yvan and
Margaret de Quay for their encouragement during the
preparation of this book.
Thanks also to Noreen Smith of Willow Trees Nursery,
Newchapel Road, Lingfield, Surrey.

Contents

INTRODUCTION 7

LADY ISOBEL BARNET 12 • TENNESSEE WALTZ 12

LA CAMPANELLA 15 • GOLDEN ANNIVERSARY 15

HAWKSHEAD 16 • DEVONSHIRE DUMPLING 16

PHYLLIS 19 • SWINGTIME 19

MICKY GOULT 20 • BLUSH O' DAWN 20

TRUMPETER 23 • ANNABEL 23

FLASH 24 • MARINKA 24

LORD LONSDALE 27 • BICENTENNIAL 27

WAVENEY GEM 28 • LENA 28

GARDEN NEWS 31 • SNOWFIRE 31

BRUTUS 32 • ROYAL VELVET 32

LADY THUMB 35 • IGLOO MAID 35

LINDA GOULDING 36 • SOUTHGATE 36

LYES UNIQUE 39 • DANCING FLAME 39

CHECKERBOARD 40 • CELIA SMEDLEY 40

ABBÉ FARGES 43 • PEPPERMINT STICK 43

OTHER FELLOW 44 • APPLAUSE 44

TING-A-LING 47 • THALIA 47

FUCHSIA SOCIETIES 48

SPECIALIST NURSERIES 48

Introduction

The fuchsia was first brought to Europe from Tropical America in the seventeenth century, and the genus named after the sixteenth-century German herbalist and botanical illustrator, Leonhart Fuchs. The earliest hybrids, bred from species imported from the Americas, date from the end of the eighteenth century, but the popularity of fuchsias in the 1880s led to many new varieties being produced. Since then, work on hybridization has advanced rapidly, and today fuchsias are cultivated in many parts of the world.

The varieties selected for inclusion from the 2,000 or so in cultivation today (some 10,000 are listed), have been chosen for their overall quality, and as representing a good cross-section of the colours, sizes, shapes and habits available. They include upright, trailing and hardy perennial forms. Each has been painted from life, and is reproduced lifesize.

I have used 'variety' as a synonym for 'cultivar'. By 'corolla' is meant the 'skirt' of the flower; 'sepals' indicate the outer parts of the flower. In some parts of the fuchsia-growing world, 'hardy' means able to withstand heat; here I have used it exclusively to mean able to withstand frost in winter. The varieties chosen should be widely available throughout the UK, North America and Australasia. However, in some cases alternative varieties which may be easier to obtain in other areas have been given.

Genii, a lovely yellow-leaved winter-hardy variety

THE VERSATILITY OF FUCHSIAS

Fuchsias can be used for a wide variety of purposes: in the garden (permanently, or as bedding plants), in the greenhouse or conservatory, in lath houses (shade houses), in baskets, wall baskets or tubs. They can be grown as hedges, standards, wall-plants, pillars or shrubs. They come in all sizes, from the tiniest species to huge modern hybrids, and in a wide range of colours – with the notable exception of yellow. There are tiny ground-hugging plants; compact upright growers for window boxes; vigorous upright bushes for tubs and troughs; large shrubs for the garden border; trailing forms; lax semi-trailing bushes; plants suitable for standards; dark-leaved Triphylla types with tubular flowers; coloured- or variegated-leaved forms; and of course the original species, including F. magellanica, the hardiest of all.

In temperate climates, the natural flowering period covers the summer months; in favoured areas in hotter climates, flowering may continue for around ten months of the year. As a general rule, the smaller-flowered the variety, the sooner it will come into bloom and the more flowers it will carry.

CULTIVATING YOUR FUCHSIAS

Fuchsias are mostly half-hardy perennial sub-shrubs, though some are hardy enough to survive outdoors during the winter. They will grow almost anywhere, except in deep shade, and plants will last for many years. However, they will do best in temperate conditions where there is some humidity, and in a filtered light. A partially shaded spot outdoors is ideal in the summer. In the hotter parts of the world, a lath

Daisy Bell, a pretty American small-flowered trailer

house will provide the best conditions for growth.

Fuchsias need five things in balance in order to thrive: water, light, air, food and warmth. In the summer, these elements will be required in quantity for active growth; in the winter, when light is naturally reduced, dormant plants will need less water, air and warmth, and virtually no feeding.

As a general rule of thumb, pale-leaved or variegated varieties need considerably less water than dark-leaved varieties. (They also tend to be more attractive to whitefly!) If the atmosphere is very damp and humid, stem-rot can be prevented or controlled in these varieties by increasing ventilation and removing any dead or dying leaves as soon as they appear. Similarly, pale-flowered varieties do best in shade (the flowers tend to redden in the sun), whilst orange-flowered varieties keep their colour best in full sun.

Grow fuchsias in a free-draining compost with plenty of humus, and feed little and often with a high nitrogen feed during active growth, and a high potash feed during flowering. They need plenty of water at this time, but good drain-

Billy Green, a pinkish-salmon Triphylla type, with upright growth and olive-green foliage

age is essential to prevent the roots from drowning.

There are three main ways to grow fuchsias: from current season's cuttings; from rested plants; or on a biennial system. Cuttings taken in the spring of the same year will make small flowering plants later in the summer; rested plants (pruned hard back and re-potted in the spring) will flower again; plants grown on a biennial system are grown on from spring cuttings, pinched out throughout the summer to produce a good plant and prevent flowering, and kept growing in a frost-free environment throughout the winter so as to make large specimen plants for flowering in the second year.

Whichever method you choose, carefully pinch out the growing tips each time two or three new pairs of leaves have appeared, to make the plant bushy and to increase the number of flowers. Discontinue pinching out about two months before flowering is required.

To make a standard, remove the sideshoots that develop in each leaf axil (the leaves will fall off naturally in due course), and at the required height leave three or four sets of sideshoots to form the head. Then pinch out the tips.

PLANTING OUT

When bedding out fuchsias for the summer, plant them with the top of the compost slightly below ground-level. When planting out hardy fuchsias to overwinter, leave a shallow saucer about 18 in/45 cm across and 5 in/8 cm deep around the stem; fill this in at the end of the season to protect the rootball from frost.

For baskets, line 12 in/30 cm containers with sphagnum moss in early spring, fill with any good soilless compost, and plant up with five plants of the same variety.

PROPAGATING YOUR FUCHSIAS

Fuchsia cuttings strike easily, especially in spring. Peat and sand mixed in equal quantities provide a good medium, and a bottom heat of around 65°F/18°C helps. Take strong fresh growth about 1 in/2.5 cm long, with two pairs of leaves. Spread the compost in a shallow tray, make holes with a dibber and firm the cuttings in gently. Spray with tepid water several times a day, and keep shaded. Roots will form in ten to fourteen days, when cuttings can be potted up individually into small pots. Resist the temptation to pot up into larger containers too quickly.

FURTHER ADVICE

I hope this book will encourage you to start growing, or to grow more, fuchsias. Specialist fuchsia nurseries (some of which are listed on page 48) are invariably helpful, as are other growers. Fuchsias are best bought from a specialist fuchsia nursery; look for a plant that is short, stocky and obviously thriving. Your national fuchsia society can provide addresses of local societies, and annual fuchsia shows often have the latest varieties on display.

Lady Isobel Barnet

◁ A British introduction, raised in 1968, this is one of the more floriferous fuchsias. The medium upright bushy growth virtually disappears under the large quantity of flowers produced. Individual flowers, which are generally held semi-erect, have an open corolla of rose-purple with flushes of imperial-purple darkening towards the edge. The sepals are rosy red. One unusual aspect of this variety is the large number of flowers produced at each leaf axil. Best colour develops if grown in a semi-shaded spot; the blooms tend to redden if it is grown in full sun. This variety responds particularly well to heavy feeding. Probably best grown as a bush, but it will also make a nice standard. Widely available.

Tennessee Waltz

▷ One of the best American winter-hardy varieties, this medium- to large-flowered Californian variety has been around for over forty years. It has self-branching upright growth, and is particularly suitable for a large bush or standard. It is very easy to grow. The double corolla is lilac-lavender splashed rose-madder. The sepals are rose-madder. Widely available.

La Campanella

▷ This superb British introduction dates from 1968 and has become the standard by which 'purple and white' basket varieties are measured. Freely available, it is an exceptionally easy and fast-growing variety. The semi-double corolla is magenta ageing to lavender. The sepals are white, slightly flushed pink. Extremely floriferous. Equally good as a large basket or a wall-basket. It looks a little spindly when young, and looks best when several plants are used together. Once established, it responds well to frequent pinching.

Golden Anniversary

◁ Named in 1979 to celebrate the fiftieth anniversary of the American Fuchsia Society, this Californian introduction is very showy. The large double flowers are produced on vigorous self-branching lax growth, which makes it particularly suitable for baskets. The corolla is intense black-purple, fading to royal purple with maturity. It has flaring petals which fade from dark to pale pink, and pink-flushed white pointed sepals. Fresh growth is very light, almost a green-gold, which fades to light green. It gives best results when grown in a sheltered spot, and it should be watered sparingly.

Hawkshead

◁ A very popular British introduction from some thirty years ago, this one is a seedling from *F. magellanica* 'Alba' (syn. *F.m. molinae* or 'Maiden's Blush'), which is one of the hardiest species available; sometimes incorrectly sold as 'Snow White'. Like its parent, it has small single flowers, but they are paler and more plentiful. The barrel-shaped corolla is white, faintly tinged with pink. The sepals are white, flushed green. The strong upright bushy growth responds well to pinching out. Readily available.

Devonshire Dumpling

▷ This recent British introduction has become extremely popular, though it is not yet freely available world-wide. The very large double flowers are at their best when the plant is grown outdoors in a shaded and sheltered spot. The corolla is white, and the outer petals are flushed pink. The sepals are neyron-rose, tipped green. It is suitable both for a large basket or a large bush, though it will require some support due to the abundance of large heavy blooms produced. Extra care is needed to avoid over-watering when young. 'So Big' is the nearest American variety; although larger, it carries less bloom.

Phyllis

▷ A superb strong-growing winter-hardy variety, 'Phyllis' is a British introduction from 1938. It has smallish semi-double flowers, produced in abundance. The corolla is rosy cerise, and the sepals are waxy rose flushed cerise. Instead of the normal four sepals, it occasionally produces up to six or seven. If used for permanent planting, it will quickly reach 48 in/120 cm. It is fairly easy to produce a large standard, and is favoured for this reason, particularly by beginners. It will also make a good large pot plant very quickly.

Swingtime

◁ If the average gardener were asked to name a red and white fuchsia, the answer would invariably be 'Swingtime'. This American variety has a double corolla of sparkling white, with pink veining and shiny red sepals. The large flowers are freely produced. Probably the best of the 'red and whites'. Being fairly vigorous, it is easy to grow, and easy to propagate. It makes a superb large basket, pillar, standard, or bush (with some support), and is universally available. Should be in every fuchsia grower's collection.

19

Micky Goult

◁ A British introduction from the early 1980s, 'Micky Goult' has quickly become a favourite. It is best as a bush or small standard, being short-jointed and fairly compact. The single corolla has mallow-pink petals. Sepals are light pink, toning to deeper pink, and tipped green. The flowers, which are produced in abundance, are generally held semi-erect. Best colour is produced if it is grown in the shade. It will flower fairly early in the season, and grows into a compact bushy plant. If 'Micky Goult' is unavailable, try 'Pink Darling' or 'Eleanor Leytham'.

Blush o' Dawn

▷ A most attractive fuchsia, 'Blush o' Dawn' likes to grow as it wishes and not always as you want it to! Raised in America over thirty years ago, it still stands out from the crowd. The double corolla is silver-grey and lavender-blue; the sepals are waxy white, with undersides tinged with pink and pointed green. It is a beautiful cultivar, and can be very versatile – I have grown it as a bush (with supports), a smallish basket, and (occasionally!) as a small weeping standard. If unavailable, try 'Impulse' or 'Silver Dawn', both of which have similar flowers, though 'Silver Dawn' is more vigorous.

Trumpeter

▷ An American introduction from almost half a century ago, this variety is very different from all other fuchsias. It is a Triphylla type fuchsia but, unusually, a trailing variety. Its spreading, cascading growth makes it very suitable for basket-work. The largish flowers are pale geranium-lake, with long thick tubes. Distinctive foliage is rich bluish-green. Widely available.

Annabel

◁ A British introduction from 1978, this is one of the best of the newer fuchsias. Its very full large double corolla is a rich creamy white, veined green and pink, and the sepals are white, flushed with pale neyron-rose. The distinctive foliage is a very attractive pale yellowish-green. 'Annabel' is one of the most free-flowering large-flowered doubles in its colour class. It is fairly vigorous and is ideal for all forms of training – I find it best as a large bush or standard, but I have also seen superb specimens of it as baskets and fans. It is widely grown, and well worth tracking down. Try 'Nancy Lou' (one of 'Annabel's' parents) or 'Roy Walker' if unavailable.

Flash

◁ Thought to date back to the 1930s, this American introduction has become a favourite wherever fuchsias are grown. The flowers are small but produced in abundance. The single corolla is light magenta-red, and the sepals are light magenta. It is frost-hardy in many areas, and takes sun and heat as well. The small foliage is light green. With its vigorous growth, 'Flash' excels as a medium to large stiff upright bush. It is too vigorous to spend its life under glass, and will respond to heavy pinching out and potting on early in the season; this will result in a huge plant smothered in bloom during the summer. Widely available.

Marinka

▷ An excellent French variety from almost a hundred years ago, 'Marinka' is extremely versatile. It is probably one of the most widely grown fuchsias in the world. Almost always grown as a basket, it will also make a superb weeping standard. A very vigorous grower, and easy to propagate, it has beautifully formed small to medium-sized flowers. The single corolla is dark red and the sepals are rich red.

Lord Lonsdale

▷ Raised in Britain over fifty years ago, this fuchsia has the most unusual peachy orange single flowers, with light apricot sepals. On young plants the leaves look quite crinkled; as the plants grow this becomes much less obvious; and when the plant is in bloom it is hardly noticeable. With canes to support its lax bushy habit, it can be grown as a large spreading bush. Best colour of bloom will be achieved in a sheltered spot in bright sunlight. 'Aurora Superba' (syn. 'Aurea Superba') is remarkably similar.

Bicentennial

◁ Named to mark the American bicentennial celebrations, this 1976 American introduction is one of the very few good 'oranges'. The centre of the double corolla is magenta, while the outer parts of each petal are streaked Indian-orange. The sepals are salmon-orange outside and slightly darker inside. The flowers develop brightest colouring when the plant is grown in full sun. In habit it is a trailer, but is less vigorous than some. With care and perseverance it makes a very attractive small standard. If unavailable, try 'Dancing Flame'.

Waveney Gem

◁ A fairly recent British introduction, 'Waveney Gem' will make a good basket or small weeping standard. It also makes a good bush, but will require support. The flowers are single; the corolla is pink flushed mauve, and the sepals are white. This variety starts blooming very early in the season, and so many individual flowers are produced that the foliage almost disappears from view. It is easy to propagate, and has a vigorous growth habit. Well worth tracking down.

Lena

▷ Introduced in Britain over a century ago, 'Lena' is found wherever fuchsias are grown, and is frost-hardy in many areas. A semi-double, it is extremely floriferous. The corolla is rosy magenta, paling at the base of the petals, and splashed with pink. The sepals are pale flesh-pink. Whilst capable of every form of training, 'Lena' excels as a vigorous basket. It is very easy to train, and, responding to frequent pinching, will make a large plant very quickly. It is also particularly easy to propagate, which may well go some way to explain its continued popularity. 'Eva Boerg', 'Elsa' or 'Hapsburgh' would be alternatives if 'Lena' is unavailable.

Garden News

▷ A showy double-flowered British variety, 'Garden News' is a colour break in frost-hardy bush fuchsias with medium-sized flowers. The corolla is magenta-rose blending to salmon-rose at the base. The sepals are frosty rose-pink. It grows into a large vigorous upright spreading bush, and is best given some support. This variety usually carries four or more blooms at each leaf joint. The bushiness of the growth is aided by its self-branching habit. A relatively recent introduction, from 1978, it is well worth tracking down.

Snowfire

◁ A Californian introduction from 1978, this unusual fuchsia has extremely showy large double blooms. The corolla is shaded from bright pink to coral, and has attractive white streaks in varying patterns on the petals. The sepals are white, tipped green. In its first year it will produce a smallish bush with a reasonable number of flowers, but it will make a much larger plant, with a lot more blooms, in its second year, and will respond well to training. It produces its best colour when grown in shade. Widely available.

Brutus

◁ A French introduction dating back to 1897, this one has certainly stood the test of time. The single corolla is rich dark purple, and matures to a reddish-purple. The sepals are rich cerise. A strong bushy upright grower, and very easy to train, it makes a very good fairly large bush or standard, or even a large pyramid. It is frost-hardy in temperate climates, and is heat-resistant in hotter zones. It propagates very easily, and is particularly recommended to the newer grower. Freely available.

Royal Velvet

▷ Raised in California in 1962, this popular fuchsia has large double blooms. The corolla starts off a vivid deep purple, gradually changing to a rich purple, with red veins at the base of the petals. Sepals are red. 'Royal Velvet' is best grown outside in a sheltered spot during the summer months. It is a vigorous self-branching variety that can be grown either as a large specimen bush, when it is at its best, or as a large standard, when care must be taken to support the weight of the many flowers carried on each branch. Widely available.

Lady Thumb

▷ Released in 1967, this hardy British introduction is a red and white sport from the universally known red and purple 'Tom Thumb'. (To complete the family, there is 'Son of Thumb', with a lilac corolla.) The small single flowers are freely produced. The corolla is white, and slightly veined carmine. Sepals are carmine. It has the dwarf upright bushy growth habit common to all members of the 'Thumb' family, and is generally available throughout Britain and Europe.

Igloo Maid

◁ This British introduction of 1972 is one of the best of the 'whites'. It has medium-sized all-white blooms, though it must be grown in the shade. Any sun, and there will be a hint of pink on the double flowers. It has yellowish golden-green foliage, which is particularly pronounced on fresh growth, but the leaves do darken with age. It will make a good medium-sized basket if pinched out well when young, and then the branches left to trail. With support, it will also make a nice bush. Another good white is 'White Galore', an American introduction with similar flowers but darker foliage.

Linda Goulding

◁ Raised in Britain recently, this variety has quickly become established as a 'banker' for exhibitors. It carries numerous small showy flowers on a good framework when trained. It makes a medium-sized upright bush. Like many of the varieties with paler-coloured flowers, it should be grown relatively 'dry' in order to avoid stem-rot. The single corolla is white veined pale pink, and the sepals are a clear pink. A good alternative is 'Countess of Aberdeen', which is white when grown in shade but goes pink in the sun.

Southgate

▷ This very versatile American fuchsia, which appeared over forty years ago, is one of the best pink doubles available. The corolla is soft powder pink and the sepals are medium pink. The largish flowers are well formed and freely produced. A fairly strong growing semi-trailer, 'Southgate' is suitable for all forms of growth, although when grown as a bush it appreciates some support. It is particularly attractive when grown as a standard, but care should be taken to support the head in its first season. In recent years its popularity has increased; it is now readily available, and widely grown. 'Ziegfield Girl' is similar but slightly less vigorous.

Lyes Unique

▷ Raised in Britain over one
hundred years ago, this was
one of the first fuchsias to have
a white tube and sepals. Very
free-flowering, it excels as
a medium upright bush.
The corolla is clear salmon-
orange, and the tube and sepals are
waxy white. Like most 'oranges', it
should be grown in the sun. Pinch out
regularly when young to encourage bushy
growth. It will require some support as it
matures. Freely available.

Dancing Flame

◁ Probably the most widely grown of the double 'oranges',
this 1981 American introduction has large showy double
flowers. The full corolla is flaming orange with a flush of
deeper orange and carmine, and a deep orange carmine
centre; the sepals are slightly paler orange. For really bright
orange flowers it must be grown in the sun. If grown in the
shade, the blooms will be nearer to salmon-pink. It makes a
spectacular basket, and produces a large quantity of flowers.
Another way of growing it is as a large bush, but you must
provide plenty of support.

Checkerboard

◁ A popular American introduction from 1948, this is a tall vigorous upright grower. For best results, keep it a little on the dry side to counteract its susceptibility to stem-rot. The medium-sized single flowers, which are freely produced, have an unusual colour combination – the corolla is red, shading to white at the base of the petals, whilst the sepals start red and change abruptly to white. If left to its own devices, a single stem will shoot up, throwing out vigorous branches like a Christmas tree as it goes. Widely available.

Celia Smedley

▷ One of the best British 'uprights', 'Celia Smedley' has been grown since 1970. It will make a huge upright bush, or a standard, in just two seasons from a cutting. For best results, pot it on fairly quickly into a large container, and keep it well pinched out (particularly when young) as it makes very heavy wood. 'Celia Smedley' is best kept growing through its first winter, particularly if a large specimen is required. The corolla is currant-red, and the sepals are neyron-rose. Its large showy flowers are freely produced. Widely available.

Abbé Farges

▷ This particularly attractive hardy French variety dates back to 1901. It has semi-double flowers, although, like many 'semi-doubles', it occasionally throws single flowers. Growth, although fairly strong, upright and bushy, is also somewhat brittle. Care should therefore be taken to avoid damaging the stems, which are easily broken. The flowers are smallish, and borne in profusion. The corolla is rosy lilac and the sepals are cerise. If treated as a pot-grown half-hardy, it will quickly produce a very large specimen, but will require some support. 'Pixie' is a similar variety that grows slightly taller than Abbé Farges, and has paler foliage.

Peppermint Stick

◁ This double-flowered American variety, raised in California in 1950, has strong upright growth. It is particularly suitable as a large bush, and can make a nice standard. The centre petals are rich royal purple, whilst the outer petals are a light carmine-rose with purple edges. The sepals are carmine, striped with white. Fairly vigorous and tall-growing, it may require some support. Ideal grown towards the back of a border. Widely available.

Other Fellow

◁ Raised in America in 1946, this very dainty small-flowered variety blooms profusely. It has upright bushy but compact growth. Usually grown as a small to medium bush, it will also make an attractive small standard. The single corolla is coral-pink, and white at the base of each petal. The sepals are waxy white, tipped green. It should be grown in the shade for best bloom colour. It is easy to grow, but keep it fairly dry to avoid the risk of stem-rot. If unavailable, try 'Mademoiselle' or 'Micky Goult'.

Applause

▷ An American introduction from 1978, this is one of the most beautiful fuchsias available today. Its growth habit is that of a reasonably strong, but not rampant, trailer. It will give best results if several plants are used when making up the basket. Large attractive double flowers are freely produced. The corolla is a deep coral and red, and the sepals are carmine. Best colour develops in the sun. If grown in the shade, the flowers are slighter lighter in colour. Be careful with the watering – this one does not enjoy being grown 'wet'. 'Marcus Graham' is a similar but slightly stiffer and more vigorous alternative.

Ting-a-Ling

▷ One of the best white varieties to date, this American fuchsia dates from 1959. The corolla and sepals are all white, and the distinctively shaped flowers are very freely produced. If grown in the sun it will, like all 'whites', develop a hint of pink. Grow it in shade for the clearest white colouring, and grow it on the dry side in order to avoid stem-rot. 'Sleigh Bells', another white, was raised by the same hybridist some five years earlier.

Thalia

◁ 'Thalia' is probably the best known of the Triphylla type of fuchsia. Its origins are somewhat obscure, but it is generally accepted that it is a German introduction from around the beginning of the century. One of the few fuchsias to be found throughout the fuchsia-growing world. The rich orange-scarlet tubed flowers are abundantly produced in terminal racemes. It has attractive dark olive-green foliage. Best results will be achieved by growing it as a bush in the sun.

Fuchsia Societies

British Fuchsia Society, Mr R. Williams, 20 Brodawel, Llannon, Llanelli, Dyfed SA14 6BJ, Wales, UK

American Fuchsia Society, San Francisco County Fair Building, 9th Avenue & Lincoln Way, San Francisco, California 94122, USA

North-West Fuchsia Societies, Mr O. de Graff, 11705 – SE, 93rd Street, Renton, WA 98056, USA

Australian Fuchsia Society, Box 97 P.O., Kent Town, South Australia 5071, Australia

Specialist Nurseries

BRITAIN
Fuchsiavale Nurseries, Worcester Road, Torton, Kidderminster, Worcs DY11 7SB

Oldbury Nurseries, Brissenden Green, Bethersden, Kent TN26 3BJ

Arcadia Nurseries, Brasscastle Lane, Nunthorpe, Middlesbrough, Cleveland TS8 9EB

Jackson's Nurseries, Clifton Campville, Nr Tamworth, Staffordshire B79 0AP

AMERICA
Regine's Fuchsia Gardens, 32531 Rhoda Ln., Fort Bragg, California CA 95437

Antonelli Brothers, 2545 Capitola Road, Santa Cruz, CA 95062

Ron and Fay Spidell's Delta Farm & Nursery, 3925 North Delta Highway, Eugene, OR 97401